thx thx thx

thx thx thx

thank goodness for everything

LEAH DIETERICH

Andrews McMeel
Publishing, LLC

Kansas City • Sydney • London

Andrews McMeel Publishing, LLC
an Andrews McMeel Universal company
1130 Walnut Street, Kansas City, Missouri 64106

www.andrewsmcmeel.com

11 12 13 14 15 TEN 10 9 8 7 6 5 4 3 2 1

ISBN: 978-1-4494-0294-5

Library of Congress Control Number: 2010937878

All photos by John Houck

ATTENTION: SCHOOLS AND BUSINESSES
Andrews McMeel books are available at quantity discounts with bulk purchase for educational, business, or sales promotional use. For information, please e-mail the Andrews McMeel Publishing Special Sales Department: specialsales@amuniversal.com

For JOHN

Dear READER OF THIS BOOK,

Thanks for picking it up. I realize a book of thank-you notes could come off as overly sentimental, syrupy even, so I applaud you for being less cynical than the average person. I might have passed over it myself.

A few years ago, I was living in the future. Not in a sci-fi kind of way, but in that I spent a lot of time thinking about what I'd do when this or that happened, or what I'd do if it didn't. It was stressful to live like that all the time. There were occasions, however, when I felt more calm, more satisfied, and I noticed these were the moments I stopped to think about all the things I had right then and there. The things I was grateful for. Being a dutiful thank-you note writer, I wrote letters to these things, no matter how small or odd they were, and saved them in a little box. First it was occasional, but in the fall of 2009 I began doing it as a daily practice.

David Foster Wallace once said he believed that sincerity would be the next literary rebellion. As a person seeking permission from people I admire, I must say I feel validated by this approval. It's true that in the snark-saturated media landscape, my growing pile of thank- you notes had begun to feel almost subversive. But as cool as feeling subversive is, there was something else I was feeling. I can't describe it in any other way than "more alive."

I decided to share the notes with a friend. She read them all and said, "You need to show these to more people." So I put them on the Internet. And people saw them, and they told me the notes made them think about things they were grateful for in their own lives. They were excited about them, and so was I. So am I. I hope that you find the same excitement in the things around you and that this book has a small part in it.

All the best,
LEAH DIETERICH

Dear Words,

Thank you for letting me make art with you. I can't really draw well, so you're a big help. See you soon.

♡, Leah

Dear Songs I'm Embarrassed to Like,

Thanks for making times when I'm alone at home or in my car that much more delicious. I'll sing you at the top of my lungs and get that amazing guilty pleasurable feeling that's hard to come by without chocolate, drugs, or alcohol. Love you! Leah

Dear headache,

Thanks for reminding me that it's unwise to drink whiskey in bed while reading right before going to sleep. It's not the best idea, and without your thumping, aching gift, I probably would do it more often. Which isn't good. Thanks again.

leah

Dear "th" sound,

Thanks for making Spanish so sweet and vulnerable sounding. I've only seen you as a speech impediment in English, but you make Spanish sexier than I would have guessed, so for _that_ and _this_, I _thank_ you. ♡, Leah

Dear Cars,

   Without your back-killing
uncomfortableness and tendency
for congregation on the various
thoroughfares of Los Angeles,
riding my bike wouldn't be nearly
such a treat. Thanks again,
                         Leah

Dear People,

Without you there would be no treat to solitude. I need you more than you know. But your mere existence also allows for the deliciousness of your opposite. Thank you for being there.

♡, Leah

Dear Dice,
Thank you for feeling so good in
my hand and for showing me
so many different possible
outcomes. You've taught me a
lot about chance and probability,
and you look pretty sitting on
my bookshelves. That's where
you'll stay. ♡, leah.

Dear Understanding,

You have kindly maintained residence in John for as long as I've known him.

Please never move. I'm sure I'll see you again soon.

Love Always, Leah

Dear Rice,

Thanks for revealing your mysterious preparation to me. I know I've burned you in the past, pretty much every time, but suddenly I feel like we get each other, and now I can make you whenever. You taste so good. Thanks again,

Leah

Dear California,

Thanks for continuing to prove everyone wrong. Your beauty is in your confusion, imperfection, improbability, and acceptance. You set a good example for the rest of us. Love you and thanks again. Leah

Dear tiny hairs,

Thanks for being so satisfying to pluck. you help me not want to pick at other stuff on my face.

Cheers,

leah

Dear Opposites,

When I'm sad you remind me that there is happiness. Darkness, and then light. You make existence have order for me. You provide eternal reassurance. You also inspired an amazing Paula Abdul song with an animated cat dancing on the stairs.

Thanks, Leah

Dear Italy,

Thanks for taking care of her
for a week. It's really nice of
you to be such a convenient place
for her and her mother and
sister to meet up. Hopefully you'll
show her a good time and make
her happy. Much love and thanks.
           -leah

thank you.

Dear patience,

I can't write about you without thinking of Guns N Roses unfortunately, but none the less, I'm happy we're getting to know each other better recently. Waiting has never been my strong suit, so I appreciate you coming into my life as I wait for someone to have their time and do the things that they need to do. Speak soon - Leah

Dear Ovulation,

Although you mark the beginning
of the descent into crampiness
and crabiness that is to come
later in the month, you are the time
of the month when I'm most horny,
and for that you are the greatest
gift of all. Thanks, Leah

Dear Bee who stung me in Joshua Tree,

I went 29 years without ever being stung. I was always so afraid of what would happen if I was, until you crawled up the back of my shorts and stung me. Now I'm not as worried about it, you bastard. Regards, Leah

Dear Knuckles, Toes, and Back,
Thanks for making sounds I
can also feel. Kind of a rare
and wonderful thing to have
those two sensations happen
simultaneously.
                    cheers,
                         leah

Dear Bee that stung me on the beach,

Thanks for being less painful than the first bee that stung me. Now I've had two bee stings in the span of 3 months, whereas I'd had none in 29 years. A character in one of my favorite books stings herself w/ bees on purpose, and your sting reminded me of that, so thx for that too. Cheers, leah

Dear words like "disappointed" and "unnecessary,"

I'm pretty cocky about how good of a speller I am, but you always trip me up. Thanks for humbling me.

Cheers,
Leah

Dear Antonioni,

Thanks for making gorgeous New Wave films that don't make me fall asleep like Godard films.

Best,
Leah

Dear Books,

Thanks for giving us a
reason to find a place to call
our own where we can build
shelves for you and build structure
for ourselves.

I'll love you always,

Leah

Dear Katie,

Thanks for being the only person I've met who also consistently sings the instrumental parts of songs. The sustained guitar in November Rain was kind of a huge bonding moment for us and a test of our collective lungs. ♡you, Leah

Dear People Who Get It,

Youre rare and wonderful and make me feel like I'm not crazy. So thanks for that. Hope I can return the favor. Love,

Leah.

Dear New York,

Thanks for making such a
fine mistress. I've been
married to Los Angeles for quite
a while now, and you provide
a great escape from the
monotony of my urban monogamy.

XO, leah

Dear Infinite Jest,

Thanks for being a challenge I was willing to accept. Thanks for reminding me to read you by weighing my bag. Thanks for being fun enough to make me want to "do the work" as your author intended. I love you. Thanks again. ♡, leah

Dear Creative Office Environments,
Thank you for letting me get away with dirty clothes and hair at the office. I also quite appreciate the opportunity to curse at will and send emails with pictures of genitalia to coworkers without any reservation.
cheers!   leah

Dear Half-Dead Plants on my deck,

Thank you for reminding me
why I am really not ready
for a pet of any kind.
Keep it real.

— Leah

Dear Fog,

If you didn't come rolling in to LA some afternoons, I'd probably always be warm and happy. And then I'd never get to be sad and I'd probably never feel like writing, so thank you. You're always welcome here. Love, Leah

Dear Beer I Had with Jason before
Having Dinner with John's Friends,
  You were very high in alcohol, and
I appreciate that. You let me let
my guard down enough to try
squid and clams cooked in a hotpot,
and now I'm in love with seafood.
'Til we meet again high-alcohol-
content beer, 'til we meet again...
                        ♡, Leah

Dear Cuerpo,

Thanks for being a sexier word to look at for the flesh and bone we're all made of. The French word "corps" feels too close to "corpse," and the English "body" just isn't elegant enough.

♡, Leah

Dear Movies,

Thanks for making me cry. Sometimes it's easier to let myself go in the darkness of the theatre than at home at my kitchen table, or in my bed. Somehow among strangers, in front of a giant moving image it's easier than in front of people and when there's no where to look. Thx again.

Leah

Dear Airplanes,

Thanks for the hours of uninterrupted time. I read more and write more on you than I ever will at home or anywhere else. Also, I like the way you shake me when there's turbulence. I don't get scared, I think it's kinda fun. Thanks again.

leah

Dear Lined Notebook Paper,

Thanks for lending some
superficial visual organization
to the messy tangle of
thoughts I transcribe onto you.

Love,
leah

Dear Pancakes,

Thank you for being such an efficient maple syrup carrier. You're also a pretty fantastic canvas on which to paint copious amounts of butter.
Bravo. ♡, Leah

Dear Vulnerability,

Thanks for being something I haven't really tried on before. I think you'll make a fine addition to the emotional closet.

Best,
Leah

Dear Broken Glass,
Thank you for not cutting me
this morning. You make the
best sound, and it's easier to
enjoy that musical quality you
possess when I'm not bleeding.
   Thanks again.
                    ♡. Leah

Dear Pens,

Thanks for not allowing me to hide my mistakes. I'll ~~wear~~ wear them like a badge of scribbly honor.

Love Always,
leah

Dear Don DeLillo,

   Thank you for not using email, for not having published until age 35, for having worked in advertising, and for White Noise. Basically for writing so well, it makes me tsk out loud when I'm reading to myself at home alone.

                    Best, Leah

Dear Mom,

Thank you for coming to visit, for buying me a knife to properly cut bread with, for indulging me in celebrating my half-birthday two days in a row, for not being shocked, for not giving me advice, and of course for loving me like I love you.   Always, Leah

thank you

Dear Assumptions,

Thank you for almost always being wrong. That consistency is still somehow surprising to me, and that in itself is rather enchanting. Thanks again. Best,

Leah

Dear Pianist,

Thanks for being one of the only words I cringe at saying out loud. Not a lot embarasses me, so good for you. You win.

Cheers! Leah

Dear Back of my Hand,

Your skin is smooth like paper and great for To Do lists. Thank you for being better than any electronic reminder device I've ever tried.

Best, Leah

Dear Body Hair,

Thanks for reminding me
I'm an animal. I can embrace
my wildness better when I
accept you, and that's awesome,
cuz I like an excuse for
wildness. Much love, Leah

Dear Handmade Cards,

Thanks for being an indicator of whether someone is awesome or not. You helped John make a great first impression on me 10 years ago, and you were my favorite gift this Xmas. I hope you enjoy hanging with your handmade-card brethren in my plastic storage box under the bed.

XO, Leah

Dear Addresses that Involve Fractions,

1223 1/2, 472 3/4 ... your diminutive stature as the location of someone's living quarters always feels whimsical, and your capacity for magic much more likely. Thanks for making my imagination kick in. Best, Leah

Dear You,

Thanks for sticking with me
even if I'm constantly shifting.
You have a knack for standing
on uneven ground, and I
appreciate it. I love you.

♡, leah

Dear Future,
   Thank you for only existing
in my mind. You're a lot
less scary when I realize
you're just make-believe.
See you when I see you.
       Best, Leah

Dear Three Different Trash Trucks
That Go Down My Alley Every
Tuesday Morning,

   I don't understand why just one
of you doesn't collect all the trash
in our alley, but thanks for being
a mystery I'll never figure out.
I'm ok with that, and thanks
for inspiring me to be more ok
with that in general. Best, leah

Dear People Who Don't Get it,

You make me explain my ideas more clearly, and sometimes that helps me understand them better too. So thank you for that.

All the best,
Leah

Dear Other People's Expense Account Alcoholic Beverages,

Thank you for being so easy to say yes to. It's nice not to have to make decisions.

cheers, Leah

Dear Farts,

Thanks for being so funny.

Love,
Leah

Dear Ocean,

Thank you for being so scary and overwhelming that I can't worry about trivial things when I'm in you. It's nice to have a break from that bullshit.

Love, Leah

Dear Cold,

Thanks for coming on before my vacation rather than during it. It's been a while since we've seen each other, hope you have a quick trip out of my body. Cheers. Leah

Dear Certain Pictures of Women Smoking,
Thank you for being so hot.
It makes absolutely no sense
why I find you attractive when
I intellectualize it, but I like
the fact that there are some
things in the world I'll never
make sense of by using my
brain. Best, Leah

Dear Honey,

Thank you for soothing my throat when I'm sick and my ears when someone calls me you. All the best,

Leah

Dear Dishes in my sink,
Thanks for giving me a task
to do while I'm procrastinating
some other task. I always
feel accomplished after I wash
you, even though I'm putting
off something else. Thanks again.
— Leah

Dear current toilet paper,
Thank you for being just the
right softness. Not too thick
like a linty sweater, and not
too thin like party decoration
crepe paper. You are the Goldilocks
and the three bears "just right"
of toilet papers. See you soon
and thanks again. Best, Leah

Dear Hope,

Thank you for being alive
and such.

Best,
leah

Dear Conference on Intersectionality,
I did not attend you, nor do I really
understand what you are about, but
I thank you for being the reason
Patrick came to LA to stay with me.
You have facilitated the catapulting
of our acquaintancehood to full-
blown friendship. I really can't
thank you enough. Much Love,
Leah

Dear Odd-Shaped Bruise on my Thigh,
Thank you for likely being the
result of sleeping on the hard
ground while camping on the
beach. You make a much better
story than just that I bumped
into the corner of a table or
something. Cheers, Leah

Dear Mornings I Don't Set My Alarm,

You are the only time I remember my dreams. Especially the sexy ones. I wish I could see you more often. Let's try to find a way to make that happen.

Love Always, Leah

Dear Guardrail on the Side of the
Road from the Guadalajara Airport
to the City,
Thanks for being in the shade and
therefore a relatively nice place
to chat with Antonio while we
waited to see if the truck would
start back up. Best wishes,
                                    Leah

Dear Air,

Thank you for smelling
like cookies right now.

All my love,
   Leah

Dear Man Who Punched out the Back
Windshield of a Mini Cooper in
Mexico City,

Thanks for acting out your macho road-
rage 5 feet in front of us, for
providing me with enough danger and
violence to shake me up and give
me a good story to tell, but for not
being disturbing enough to give me
nightmares. Thanks also for reminding
me yet again to never give people the
finger while I'm driving. Take it easy.
                                    —Leah

Dear Blood I Just Spit in the Sink,
Thanks for reminding me that I
can't stop flossing my teeth for
two weeks and assume it's no
big deal. Your redness says
I must floss regularly. Thanks
bloody spit. Point taken.
XO, leah

Dear Lovely Lady I've Never Met,
Thanks for convincing John that
V-Neck t-shirts look good on him
and that his chest hair is sexy.
He wouldn't believe me, but I'm
glad he believed you! Cheers to
that. All the best, Leah

Dear Tears,

Thank you for staying at bay the last few weeks. We were **seeing** a whole lot of each other, and your absence is welcomed because it makes my heart grow fonder for you. Next time you fall from my eyes and splash my collarbones, I'll see you as more of a treat.

Til then, leah

Dear Your Thoughts,

Thank you for being with me. There are a lot of places they could be, and I appreciate their pointing in my general direction. I'm thinking about you too. Love Always, Leah

Dear Rainbows,

Thanks for being the gayest of all weather phenomena~~s~~.

Always happy to see you.
Brings a smile to my face.

XO, leah

Dear Meeting,

Thank you so so so so much
for being over. You're
beautiful when you're over.
Don't change a thing.

Best, Leah

Dear Men's Undershirts,

Thank you for having a greater ability to get old and soft than other types of t-shirts. If only your lovely tactile qualities weren't accompanied by yellowed armpits, but then again no one's perfect, and you're pretty close. XO, Leah

Dear Uncertainty,

Thanks for also essentially being possibility. I'm a lot more into you when I think of you that way.

All the best,
Leah

Dear Curse Words + Dirty Words,

Thanks for consistently being fun to say. Few words feel as good coming out of my mouth. Cheers,

Leah

Dear She,

Thank you for also containing the word "he". It just reaffirms my belief that we can all have both coexist inside ourselves, as you do.

much love, Leah

Dear Cities with Good Public Transit,

Thanks for making it so much more fun and easy to go out and get a little drunk.

Best Wishes,
Leah

Dear People Who Walk Slow in Front
of Me and Block the Whole Sidewalk,
Thank you for on rare occasions
noticing that you are indeed
creating a sidewalk traffic jam
and offering to let me pass. Most
people lack this awareness
and consideration. So refreshing.
        cheers, leah

Dear Anything I've lost and then Found,
Thanks for reminding me that even
if something seems completely gone,
and I've stopped looking for it long
ago, that it can magically materialize,
usually in the pocket of a winter coat
or something. So even though I've been
told I might get lost along the way
as new avenues are explored, you
give me faith that I too might get
found again, in some pocket, in
some other season. Much love, Leah.

Dear Continuums,

Thanks for being a soothing range, span, or variegation and for being an alternative to the harshness of black and white. Binary is for computers, and I'm a human.

much love, Leah

Dear Turntable/Speakers/Vinyl Records,
Thanks for being so expensive I can
resist a potentially obsessive and
pricey new collecting hobby. Your
cost prohibition will do wonders
for the preservation of clutterlessness
in my home. I still love you though.
Like the Ewok Village when I was
little, I'll just have to play with you
at other people's houses. See you—
                                        Leah

Dear Steering Wheel,

Thanks for being an
awesome pad for air drumming.

XO, Leah

Dear Virgin America In Flight Music Library,
Thank you for having Nirvana's
song "Rape Me." Out of Nirvana's
sizeable catalog of alt-nineties
hits, you chose to include this,
my most favorite, despite its
potentially offensive title. That
takes balls. Bravo.

All the best, Leah

Dear Surf Movies,
Thank you for being so amazing
I don't close my mouth for
an hour and a half. I grind
my teeth quite a bit normally,
so you're an excellent reprieve.
Cheers, Leah

Dear White Noise Maker,
  Thanks for lulling me to sleep
and for making me chuckle
thinking about how a comedian
could do a bit about you being
racist or something. What with
you being a "white" noise maker
and all. Good work all around.
         Best, Leah

Dear Shit,

Thanks for being a universal experience. There are so few of those. I hate to say you are the great equalizer, because then I have to ~~associate~~ associate equality with stink, but you kind of are. You kind of are. Regards, Leah

Dear Haruki Murakami,

Thanks for making me confuse your stories with my own dreams. Whenever I read one of your books, I have that perpetual "was-that-a-dream-or-real-life-or-something-I-read feeling." It's a pretty enchanting state of mind.

Thanks again, Leah

Dear Items of Your Clothing that I Wear,

Thanks for letting me be you and me at the same time. I'm not sure if it cultivates a sort of empathy, but maybe. Either way, it usually feels soft and smells good, which is nice.

much love, Leah

Dear Photographs,

Thank you for letting me stare
at people without feeling like
I'm being rude.

All the best,

Leah

Dear My Own Laziness,

Thank you for allowing the bag of clothing I was going to donate to charity to remain in the trunk of my car for so long that I'm actually into it again and want to keep them. Feels like I went on a shopping spree. Other people's laziness doesn't do much for me, but you, my own personal laziness, you're all right. XO, Leah

Dear Beat,

Thanks for never skipping
when we see each other.
Let's dance.

♡, Leah

Dear People Who Tell me to Slow Down,

Even though you're telling, you're also essentially asking me why I'm trying to rush the journey and why I think where I'm going is more important than where I am. These are good questions.

Best, Leah

Dear Five Senses,
Thank you for only existing in the present moment. I can't taste something in the future, and I can't hear something in the past. Thanks for only being accessible now. It makes you somehow precious and mundane all at the same time.

♡, Leah

Dear Jet Stream,

Thanks for taking me to him faster and for taking me away from him more slowly.

Love, Leah

Dear Goodbye,

Thank you for almost never being final. I hope to bid you two, three, four times at least. Maybe more.

All the best, Leah

Dear Piles of Books I Haven't Read,

Thanks for making me feel bad about myself for not reading fast, or enough, and for buying things before I really need them. And then, upon having those thoughts, for reminding me to stop being so god-damned hard on myself about everything. Best, Leah

Dear the words "both" and "sometimes",

Thanks for being great responses to any number of questions. I like how inclusive and noncommittal you are. I find you simply luxurious.

All the best,

Leah

Dear People that Come Over to my House,
Thank you for your visits.
Without them, I would never
clean my bathroom.

Cheers,
Leah

Dear Novocained Lip,

Thank you for not looking
like what you feel like you
look like.

Cheers,
Leah

Dear Metaphorical Book John
and I are Both Reading,

   Thanks for letting us
be on the same page.

        All the best,

            Leah

Dear My Expectations,

Thanks for being quite low. My arms aren't very long, so it's important that I can reach you, even if I have to go on tiptoe. ♡, Leah

Dear Turntable that I said I
wouldn't buy but bought anyway,

Thanks for giving me a reason to look
through records at the thrift store
down the street. Without you, I wouldn't
know that there exists a recording
of "My Fair Lady" in Hebrew. I can't
imagine NOT knowing that now. I
look forward to the many other
amazing discoveries you'll facilitate.

Love Always, Leah

Dear Printed Reading material;

Thanks for having an end.
The internet doesn't have one,
so I never know when to stop.

All the best,
Leah

Dear Any Day I Can Walk Past
a Reflective Surface and Not
Look for my Image in it,

Thanks for being rare. Like
diamonds, but better.

Best, Leah

Dear Tall Truck that Touched the Trees,
Thank you for being in front of me so
that my car was periodically showered
with Jacaranda petals, like confetti,
like a surprise party, like I won
something on a game show, over
and over and over.
                    much love,
                              Leah

Dear People Near Me Speaking
Languages I Don't Speak,

Thanks for making eavesdropping
impossible. So rare to have
someone's conversation be white
noise. I'd be able to read and
write in public much better if
everyone did as you do.

Best, Leah

Dear that Magical Hour at dusk
before people close their curtains,

Thank you for being more
captivating than TV ever could.

All the best, Leah

Dear Bird Shit,

Thank you for looking like white paint. Sidewalks would look a lot nastier were that not the case.

Cheers,
leah

Dear Certain Glasses in my Cupboard,

Thanks for making drinks taste better than they do in other glasses. There may not be a scientific explanation for this, but I don't need one.

All my best, Leah

Dear Melancholy,

Thank you for producing the best
music, writing, and art of any
of the emotions. Sometimes you
linger, and other times your visits
are short, but when you come
I always end up making something.
You're a better house guest than
sadness because you leave gifts.
♡, Leah

Dear Tea,

Thanks for being able to be decaffeinated merely by steeping you three times. If only you could show cigarettes how to be decancerated, I'd be really impressed. Best, Leah

Dear People Who Drive the new version
of the VW Bug,

Thanks for making a vehicular
statement that helps me know
we probably won't have an
incredible amount in common.
I'm busy, you're busy, and your
silly choice of car speaks volumes
and saves us both a lot of trouble.
Cheers, Leah

Dear Kindness,

   Thank you for killing people.
You're definitely my favorite
weapon. If only they made a
holster for you, perhaps I could
wield you more quickly.

      Thanks again, Leah

Dear you,

Thanks for coming back.
My life is fuller and richer
when you're in it.

♡always,

Leah.

Dear the Word "Être,"

Thanks for being the pure and undifferentiated French verb for being. You exist before any conjugations, before any subjects or objects or assigned gender. I can't think of a single-word equivalent in English. Being should be as elegant and concise as you are.

Thanks again, Leah

Dear California Rooves with no Insulation or Attics,

Thank you for providing only the bare minimum of separation between me and the rain. Makes for great sleeping, the sounds you afford.

Thanks again, Leah

Dear Hands,

Thanks for finding your
way into my pants.

Best,
leah

Dear Men Who Walk Pomeranians,

Thanks for having such a great sense of humor.

Cheers, Leah

Dear $2.00 Bills,

Thanks for being the only denomination of money that seems like it's not meant to be spent. If only every bill was so frameable or precious, my wallet would be a lot fuller.

Best, Leah

Dear Cash Register Totals
in Amounts like $19.59,

Thanks for always making
me want to say: "it was a
good year," even if I wasn't
born yet. I love anything that
compels silliness.

Love, Leah

Dear Surprising Yet Fulfilling Moments
of Human Contact,

Thanks for being so memorable. The
feeling of the doctor's assistant
making a mold of my foot for
shoe inserts, or the man's back
I touched asking if he needed
help getting his walker up the
sidewalk. Thanks for staying
with me. much love, Leah

Dear Burnt Toast,

Thanks for being I smell
I love that few others
do. Saves more smell for me.

All the best,

Leah

Dear Owls,

Thank you for being an
excellent way to date a
thrift store item like a
brooch or a dish towel.
You are the darling of 1970's -
era tchotchkes. Best, Leah

Dear Empty Bar,

People are often annoying, so thank you for not having any tonight.

Take care,

Leah

Dear Dad,

Thank you for always having awesome new reggae for me to check out when I come home. You are the most awesome near-60-year-old, non-pot-smoking skinny white man connoiseur of reggae around. Love you!

Leah

Dear Walks,

Thanks for being the activity during which I come up with my best ideas. It used to be showers, ~~that~~ but no longer. Guess ill be very creative and very fit but not so clean. C'est la vie.

XO, Leah

Dear Restraint,
   Thank you for allowing me
to refrain from asking
questions I don't need to know
the answers to, like "do you
love her?"
                    Best, Leah

Dear Clean Sheets

Thank you for feeling infinitely better than dirty ones.

All the best,

Leah

Dear Berets,

Thank you for being able to transform from french, to militant, to hippyish, with nothing more than a shift of position. If only it were that easy for people.

Best, leah

Dear World,

Thank you for not revolving around me. I get stressed out thinking that things people do or don't do, say or don't say, have directly to do with me. It's a lot of pressure. But then occasionally I remember that you're doing your own thing, and I'm a very small part, and that I certainly don't have enough mass to exert any revolutionary force on you. phew.

♡, Leah

Dear Dill,

Thanks for making things taste so good and also making me giggle. You are infinitely appealing to a refined palate and an immature mind.

Best, Leah

Dear Licked Fingertip,

Thank you for being an excellent baked-good-crumb-picker-upper.

Cheers,

Leah

Dear Free wheel on My Bike,
Thank you for sounding
like a rattle snake when
I coast. You are so badass.
   Thanks again,
                Leah

Dear Peque,

Thanks for telling me once
that I smelled like books.
Can't think of a better
compliment.

Best, Leah

Dear World Cup,

Thanks for being the
explanation for people
screaming next door.

Cheers,

Leah

Dear 3-Legged Dogs who
Don't Seem to Notice,

Thanks for being so totally
amazing and for always
lifting my spirits when I
see you trotting along.
much love, Leah

Dear People Who are Friends with
All Your Exes,

Thanks for reassuring me that
we can, in fact, be friends
in the future, even if it seems
unlikely now. By your history,
that is, not by your actions
or words. Thanks for that
history. All my love, Leah

Dear Dust,
  Thank you for responding to
almost any cleaning method.
I like that I can wipe you away
with my hand. Thanks also
for featuring so prominently
in the uber dramatic Kansas
song regarding your position in
the wind. Cheers, Leah

Dear Leah.

Thank you for being a fairly uncommon name. I never look up when someone calls out Sarah, or Kate, or Jennifer like so many of my friends do.

much love,

Leah

Dear Morning Bathroom Visit,

Thank you for making
room for breakfast.

All best, Leah

Dear Bee that Stung my Face
While I was Riding my Bike,

Thanks for choosing the
side of my face where I
already had a swollen lip
from something else. makes
icing both things at once
totally possible. Regards, leah

Dear Margin Notes,

Thanks for allowing me to look back, years later, and see what a different me thought was important, and what was worthy of underlining.

Cheers, Leah

Dear the therapists of my friends,
and lovers, and partners,

Thanks for helping them become
people I'm even more glad to
know than I already was.

much love,

leah

Dear the Sound of Someone
Sauteing as I Walked by their
window,

mmmmmm. thanks.

- Leah

Dear Astrological Signs,
Thanks for being excellent
scapegoats. I love being able
to chalk up my self-centered,
star-of-the-show tendencies
to being a Leo. Blaming stars
is convenient.

Cheers, leah

Dear People of Craigslist,
Thank you for buying our things
so we can keep our house neat
and buy different things. We
have a something in/something out
policy. and your arrival at our
door with fists full of cash
really makes that possible.
    Thanks again,   Leah

Dear Ignorance,

Thank you for your blissful gifts of unknowingness.

Best, Leah

Dear Willpower,

Thanks for being a quality I've always possessed. When you've kept me healthy and productive, I love you. When you've caused me to eat too restrictively or exercise too obsessively, I'm less fond of you. But what can I do? Like any superpower, you are my blessing and my curse, and I will try to always use you for good. much love, Leah

Dear Tree Roots that Buckle the Sidewalk,
Thanks for being a simple reminder of how much stronger nature is than us. Even if I trip over you, I have to say I'm impressed

All the best,

Leah

Dear 4th of July Houseguests,

Thank you for being a reason to purchase a tiny grill that we can use on our deck. I don't know why we always denied ourselves this simple cooking appliance, but I love that now when I ride my bike home and smell a BBQ, I can realize it's ours!

much love, leah

Dear Any Woman Who Can Make
Upper Lip Hair Sexy,

Thank you. There aren't that many
of you. Frida Kahlo, JD Samson...
You're the only ones that come to
mind, and while you don't
necessarily inspire me to stop hiding
mine, you certainly make me more
comfortable about having it in the
first place. Best, Leah

Dear Bras,

Thanks for being the one undergarment that can be worn multiple times without washing. Although I suppose I really should be thanking breasts for not being prone to stinkiness.

All the best, Leah

Dear You,

Thank you for appearing in crowds,
or walking down the street, or with
your back turned to me at a
restaurant. Even though you're
thousands of miles away, you have a
unique power to inhabit other
people's faces, and bodies, and gestures.
Even if only for a fleeting moment.

All my love, Leah

Dear Doors,

Thanks for having a way of working in concert. When one of you closes, another of you opens. You're so beautifully synchronized and choreographed, like dancers, despite being so rigid and frequently made of wood.

Best, Leah

Dear Bebop and Free Jazz,
Thanks for being some of the
first musical genres John and
I could agree on. Your atonality
actually produces a lot of
harmony between us.

Best, Leah

Dear Sidewalk Cracks,

Thank you for not breaking my mother's back when I step on you, despite rhymes warning the contrary.

Regards,
Leah

Dear single playing cards I occasionally
see lying in the street,

Thanks for making me feel lucky
in some unexplainable casino
kind of way.

All the best,

leah

Dear Armand Hammer Museum of Art,
Thanks for having a name I can adapt to the "please-hammer-don't-hurt-'em museum." Your so-called high art culture intersection with my low culture reference is so seamless and easy and fun. You have great exhibits, too. See you soon.

XO, leah

Dear Kevin,

Thanks for being an
excellent dog or bird name.

Cheers, Leah

Dear People with Strong Handshakes
and full contact hugs,

You are so welcoming and
put me at ease faster than
any words ever could.
So, thank you.

Love, Leah

Dear Erin and Ehren,

Thanks for having the same first name. It's fun to tell people my sister and her husband are both named Erin/Ehren. It's that sameness that actually makes you different.

Love you, Leah

Dear End of the Day Shadow,

Thanks for making my legs look abnormally long instead of, say, making my ass look abnormally wide. Very courteous of you.

Cheers,

Leah

Dear Dusty Trophy Shop Windows,
Thank you for always making me
feel like taking photographs of you.
I love that you consistently inspire
something other than the desire
to compete at sports. Because of
this you always remind me of
who I am, in a most satisfying way.
    Best, Leah

Dear Records,

Thanks for requiring me to listen to songs I don't love in order to hear the ones I do. I think you train me for life better than digital music, which allows me too much control, with playlists and the ability to weed out anything I don't want to hear.

XO, leah

Dear Jewelry that Doesn't say Anything about me other than "I'm wearing Jewelry Today",

Thanks for that.

Cheers,
Leah

Dear Names that Get Stuck in My Head,

Thanks for being much less maddening than songs that get stuck in my head.

Best, Leah

Dear Boy Who Occasionally Wore
Long Hippy Skirts at my high school,

Thanks for being brave and
for being one of my most
memorable crushes.

Cheers, leah

Dear Tennis Balls,

Thank you for being useful for so much more than just tennis. You make excellent dog toys, as well as covers for the bottoms of old people's walkers.

Cheers, Leah

Dear Sore Muscles,

Thanks for being a physical manifestation of a sense of accomplishment.

All the best,

Leah

Dear Girl Who Always Wears
High Tops,

Thank you for helping me
learn to love being a woman
more than anyone in heels
ever has.

much love, Leah

Dear Wall-to-wall carpeting,

Thanks for being my
floor-couch.

All the best,
leah

Dear Bourbon,

Thank you for not turning
me into the devil like vodka.

Cheers,
, leah

Dear Knots in Wood,

Thank you for sometimes looking like the eyes of animals. You remind me that trees are alive just like jaguars and elephants.

Cheers, Leah

Dear cramps,

Thanks for reminding me how great I feel during the 27 or so days a month when I don't have you. Keep up the good work.

Best, Leah

Dear Vertigo,

Thank you for going away after a few days. I couldn't have gone on stumbling around like that, feeling like I was spinning. ~~too~~ How would I know if ~~I~~ I drank too much in the future?? Phew.

Best, Leah

Dear Long Black Hair that Went to Her Waist,
Thank you for being so dark, you
absorbed light. You drew me in like
a black hole, and I had to braid you,
it was all I could think about. I'm
glad your owner didn't mind. It was
such an incredibly satisfying and intimate
experience. You slid perfectly between
my fingers as I wove. Thank you for
not tangling, as I never wanted to
hurt her.   Much love,   Leah

Dear Japanese Kimono Brand Condoms,
Thanks for being the thinnest
and best out there. I shouldn't be
surprised you're so great, after all, the
Japanese make pretty much everything
better, cars, electronics, etc. But I'm
more thankful for you because
having excellent protected sex is way
more important than watching TV
or driving. Best, Leah

Dear Hedges,

Thank you for making beautiful walls. You provide the right amount of security and privacy without looking as paranoid as concrete.

Cheers, Leah

Dear Monday,

Thanks for having the word "mon" in you. That's French for "mine", in case you weren't aware, Monday, but it makes me think of you more as "my day," and frankly that sounds like a much more promising start to the week.

Best, Leah

Dear Spanish Accented English Speakers,
Thank you for pronouncing "sheets"
and "shits" the same way, causing
one of you to write the sentence,
"She was nice and washed my
shits for me." I love this. I love
it so much. Thanks again.
                    XO, Leah

Dear Cities,

Thank you for having light pollution that prevents me from seeing the stars. This way, whenever I'm away from you, and I see how many stars are actually up there, I am literally astounded. If I saw that stellar expanse daily, it would lose impact, and I can't think of anything worse than being jaded to the universe.

All my love, Leah

Dear Scissors,

Thank you for transforming pants into shorts. You're like a very sharp magic wand that produces new items in my closet.

Best, Leah

Dear Time I Went on Vacation and Forgot to Arrange for Someone to Feed my Dog and so She Starved to Death,

Thank you for being only a dream.

Regards,

Leah

Dear Trios or Threesomes that Work,

Thank you for defying the old "three's a crowd" adage, much in the way tricycles are more stable than bikes. I have a soft spot for successful defiance.

Cheers, Leah

Dear August 8th,

Thank you for being the coolest
birthday ever. When I write you
as numerals, 8.8, then tip you on
your side ∞.∞, you are two
infinity symbols, which is basically
permission to never stop
celebrating, right? Thanks again.

Leah

Dear People With Medium Length Brown Hair Who Use My Shower,

Thank you for making it impossible to distinguish your hair from my own. Makes cleaning the drain far less gross.

Cheers, Leah

Dear Pants that look Slim but
Don't cut off the Circulation
to my crotch when I sit down,

Thank you for being comfortable
and stylish, rare and wonderful.
I'll wash you on cold and line
dry you with care. I'll treat
you right. All my love.
                    - Leah

Dear Sneezes,

Thank you for being like orgasms you can have at work.

Best, Leah

Dear Vertical Blinds,

I know I complain about how ugly and generic you are, even though I'm too lazy to change you (I don't own my apartment, so you're not really mine to change); but I have to say, when you filter morning sunlight into those perfect striped patterns on the carpet and wall and furniture, you make me really happy. Best, Leah

Dear Cereal,
Thank you for being even more delicious at night. There is something about eating you when I'm not supposed to be that ups your tastiness. I guess transgression adds flavor.
XO, Leah

Dear Imaginary Band Names,
Thanks for being the perfect receptacle for random collections of words and phrases. The implied possibility of hearing you shouted following "Ladies and Gentlemen, put your hands together for" gets me excited in a way few other word combinations can.
XO, Leah

Dear Times When I See Someone
I Kind of Know and Actually go
up to them and Say Hi Instead
of Pretending I Don't See Them
Because I'm Shy,

Thanks for making me
proud of myself.

♡, leah

Dear Story about a Friend of a Friend Who Lost His Thumb as a child and Had His Big Toe Grafted in its Place,

Thank you for being the sort of stuff that would have made me lose sleep as a kid but seems magical, comical and amusing as an adult. It's stories like you that help me realize how far I've come in terms of dealing with fear.

All the best,

Leah

Dear Fruit That's Fallen From the Tree to the Ground,

Thank you for looking gruesome and delicious. I love that you can make my skin crawl and mouth water all at once.

Love, Leah

Dear Long Distance,

Thank you for no longer existing
in terms of telephone rates,
and for allowing me to really
see someone in focus, the way
older people do with restaurant
menus held at arm's length.
                much love, Leah

Dear Everything,

Thank you for happening
for a reason.

Cheers, Leah

Dear Empty Apartment,

Thanks for not asking anything of me, not caring if I talk, if I sing, if I cook or don't cook, eat well or not. Thanks for being a space I can swim around in. I'm a bit underwater right now, but there's plenty of room to breathe in you. ♡, Leah

Dear the End of Something,

Thank you for being the
beginning of something else.

much love,
Leah

Extra thx to:

JOHN HOUCK
CHRIS SCHILLIG
KATE MCKEAN

And to my dearest family and friends:
You're too good to me; your gifts too many.
You'll keep me in thank-you notes for life.

About the Author

Leah Dieterich began thxthxthx.com in 2009. She is proud to have a story included in *Cassette from My Ex: Stories and Soundtracks of Lost Loves* (St. Martin's Press, 2009). When she's not writing thank-you notes, she can be found serving as a creative director and writer at an advertising agency in Los Angeles, California.